THE ENGLISH COUNTRY
COTTAGE

THE ENGLISH COUNTRY
COTTAGE
INTERIORS, DETAILS & GARDENS

SALLY GRIFFITHS
Photographs by BRIAN HARRISON

PHOENIX ILLUSTRATED

CONTENTS

Once the humble dwelling of labourers, artisans and craftsmen, the English country cottage has been revived as a comfortable country home for those attracted to the romance

of the rural idyll. No matter how forgotten or neglected, the cottage exercises a particular charm, representing old traditions and a way of life that has virtually disappeared.

INTRODUCTION

The collection of special English treasures that appears in the following pages has come about from my longtime fascination with the English cottage around the country – from Cumbria to Cambridgeshire and beyond. The cottages are brought to life here with the help of photographer Brian Harrison. I hope you enjoy this encounter.

Sally Griffiths

Right: *The original front door belonging to this delightful cottage in the West Country is no longer in use. Here the owner has created an interesting ensemble using an old Victorian fireplace surrounded by terracotta pots filled with geraniums. In summer the porch is virtually concealed beneath a mass of sweet smelling honeysuckle.*

Stable Cottage

LANGFORD BUDVILLE • SOMERSET

Typical oddities of England's rural social history are hidden behind the façade of this cottage. Originally built in the late 18th-century as stabling for a nobleman's horse and carriage, the structure was later converted into a pair of one-up, one-down homes – each for a dozen occupants. The building was subsequently converted again – first as a two roomed 12 × 3 m (40 × 10 feet) single storey cottage, and then about ten years ago by the present owners.

Above: *A rear view of the pink-washed cottage in its serene setting with the crenellated tower of the village church. In the background giant grey thistles (Onopordum acanthium), lavender, daisies and euphorbia flourish in borders, creating a garden ideal for both winter and summer.*

Right: *A platform bedroom has been erected at one end of the cottage over the kitchen. A 17th-century oak cupboard and a grey 1940s painted corner cupboard flank the arched kitchen opening. In the kitchen, terracotta walls and terracotta floor tiles, partly covered with an American rag rug, contrast with the matt black Rayburn stove.*

The first priority was to install a makeshift kitchen and tiny bathroom before undertaking the major renovations. The aim of the restoration was to create an unusual sense of space within the restricted limits of a cottage, and this was mainly achieved by removing the ceilings to expose the beams of the windowless attic. Some of these beams were left bare in order to emphasise the character of the building, while others which were considered too instrusive in the overall scheme, were plastered over. The internal walls flanking the fireplace were also removed to create a single, larger room with a centred fireplace and access to a small galleried bedroom at the far end of the room.

Left: *The panelling in the
sitting room was made from an
assortment of old doors painted
blue. The checked rug is
American. Curtains were
considered unnecessary for the
internal window which
overlooks the conservatory.
The sitting room opens into the
dining area where a farmer's
office cabinet is located against
the rear wall.*

Right: *The hall is virtually
dominated by the model yacht
suspended above the fireplace.
The painting beneath is by a
relative of the owners. The
wood-burning stove was made
to measure and opens on both
sides of the chimney breast. The
rattan chair, complete with
tapestry cushion, was made
by the owner. The wooden
floorboards are from a local
architectural salvage company.*

When the present owners chose to make the cottage their main residence additional rooms were needed, and an extra bedroom, bathroom and study were added. A conservatory, which connects these extensions, allows more light to enter the house as well as providing another seating area. New windows and French doors were installed, and the sitting room was also further enlarged. The spacious L-shaped reception area, panelled at one end, was floorboarded with wood reclaimed from an athletics stadium.

The colour scheme of subtle sandy tones and contrasting burnt umber adds to the lightness of the interior, and serves as a neutral background for the collection of country furniture.

The front door is concealed behind a curtain at the rear of the sitting room, and entry to the house is from the garden, where rare breeds of chicken roam among the flowers, adding to the pastoral atmosphere.

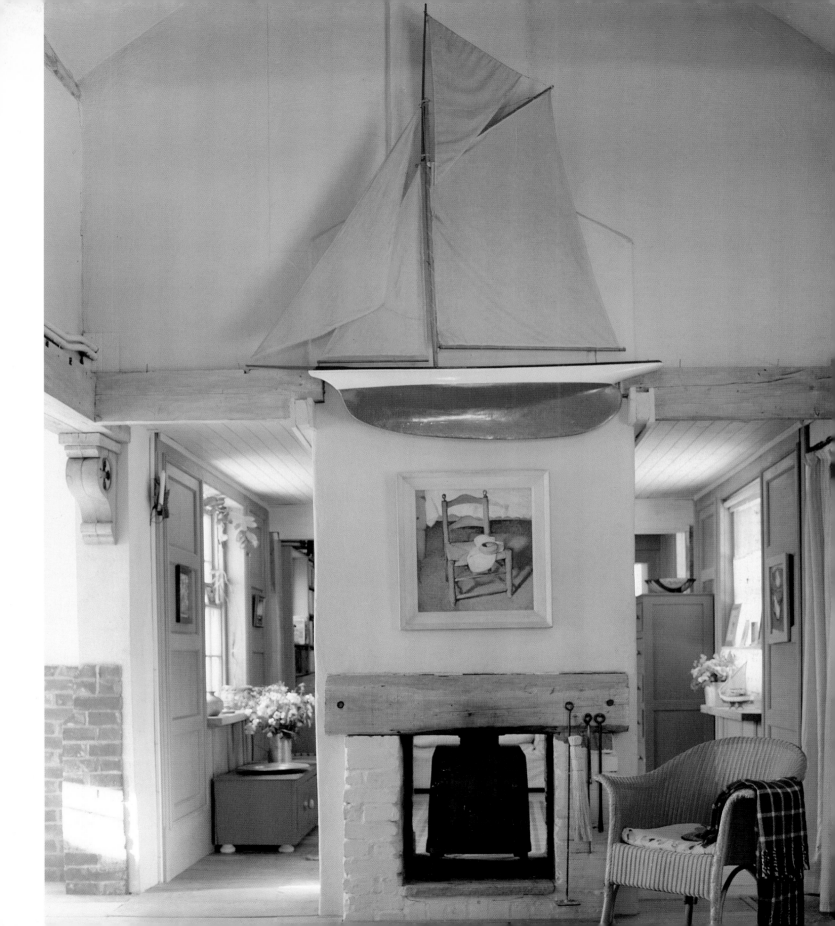

Left: *The new first floor bathroom, opening from the landing, is both simple and functional with tongue-and-groove walls and door. The cast iron Victorian bath has antique brass taps. The plain terracotta linoleum floor works well with the colour of the bath. Along the back wall a simple wooden shelf is used to display decorative accessories.*

Right: *The conservatory, a later extension, leads directly into both garden and house and was designed with these brick piers and French doors. In one corner an old Belfast sink has been added to provide water for an ever-growing collection of plants. Pink walls, pale grey-green woodwork, wooden floorboards and a white sofa are congenial neighbours, teaming well with the old slate-topped table and wrought iron French chandelier.*

Angler's Cottage

BRUTON • SOMERSET

Known locally as "The General's Cottage", due to the profession of the previous owner, this charming 16th-century timber-framed thatched cottage was derelict until bought by the present owner – an enthusiastic angler who was attracted by its proximity to the river where he fished, and by its remote, unspoiled surroundings.

Above: *View of the pretty 16th-century thatched cottage from the far side of the stream. The white woodwork offsets the brick walls, which are covered with climbing roses during the summer. The entire roof was rethatched by a local thatcher soon after its purchase.*

Right: *The French windows in the sitting-room lead into the garden. A fine 18th-century leather sofa takes pride of place in the room. Additional earlier pieces include the 16th-century Welsh dugout cupboard (corner, far right) and East Anglian table in front of the window (left).*

There were two rooms on the ground floor with a couple of outhouses tacked on to the rear. A rickety staircase led to four small rooms upstairs. There was no bathroom or cloakroom.

Apart from rethatching, no major structural alterations or additions to the cottage were necessary, but modest changes were made in order to maximize space and to suit the new owner's individual requirements.

The ceilings were raised, and the walls on either side of the fireplace taken down to create one large reception area. As a safety precaution, a new flue was inserted into the existing chimney stack: the General's highly individual but rather hazardous method of keeping a cozy fire going had

been to place a tree trunk stretching from the door to the hearth, edging it into the fire as it burned.

Upstairs, two very small bedrooms were converted into one large room with a study at one end. Custom-made bookshelves fashioned from old beams and wooden planks are a practical and decorative feature of this now-spacious room.

At the back of the house one of the remaining bedrooms was converted into a bathroom, while a small loo was created from one of the original outhouses that was now incorporated into the main structure of the house.

The cottage doors were replaced and the original windows repaired. Existing plumbing – water comes from a nearby spring – and electricity were updated. However, a telephone was considered unnecessary in a rural retreat.

The simple decor – white walls and a white painted staircase, floors of polished quarry tiles and pine shutters made from old timber – make an ideal background for the 16th-century furniture, highlighting the rare quality and superb lines of these antiques.

Above: *A view of the study, which is located at one end of the bedroom, showing the bookcase constructed of 16th-century beams and an antique Spanish walnut table with chip carving and stipple work with original ironwork handles.*

Smuggler's Haunt

NEAR LULWORTH COVE • DORSET

This 19th-century cottage, perched on top of the cliffs, was once a smugglers' hide-out; its coastal location making it convenient for clandestine activities. A trap door in the cottage floor opened into a narrow tunnel leading to a cavern from where the smugglers could reach the sea and seagoing craft.

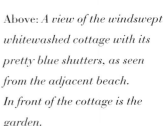

When first built around 1824, the cottage was considerably smaller than it is today, having a rear kitchen and a long narrow sitting room on the ground floor and three small bedrooms upstairs. This arrangement remained until the 1920s when the cottage was extended to provide two extra bedrooms downstairs and a bedroom and bathroom above.

The cottage had been well maintained over the years and, despite the winds and stormy seas on this part of the coast, was in good shape both externally and internally when the present owners bought it in the 1980s. The house was already known to them, having previously been owned by friends.

Before adapting the cottage to suit their needs, however, there was a more urgent problem to be addressed: the gradual erosion of the coastline. To prevent the cottage from collapse, a coat of concrete several feet thick was laid over the rocks as a precautionary measure against further crumbling.

In addition to the previous extension, a further bathroom

Above: *A view of the windswept whitewashed cottage with its pretty blue shutters, as seen from the adjacent beach. In front of the cottage is the garden.*

Left: *The far end of the sitting-room with the bay window that overlooks the beach. The room is clearly furnished for comfort. The old pine dresser is crammed with a collection of nautical memorabilia.*

Right: *Another view of the long,*
narrow sitting room which
overlooks the garden and the
bay. Given the history of the
property, the nautical theme
of the decor is appropriate.
The idea of fixing fishing rods
and oars to the beams on the
ceiling was borrowed from a
restaurant in the South-West.
Since then, colourful examples
from the south of France and
Spain have been added. The
fireplace was originally the site
of the bread oven and has been
left exactly as it was. The
decoration is simple, influenced
by the whitewashed walls and
quarry tiles. The sofa is covered
in pale blue cotton with pink
and blue cushions. Above the
sofa, blocks of ships' hulls have
been mounted and framed.

Left: *One of the children's bedrooms, decked out in red, white and blue. The pine bed has a red-and-white checked cover and the bedside table is home to model boats. The interesting and unusual collection of life-jackets echoes the nautical theme evident throughout the cottage.*

Right: *The main bedroom has high-flown windows designed for panoramic views over the beach and sea. The blue-and-white theme continues with white walls and a hand-painted stencil border of seashells picked out in blue, antique blue-and-white plates above the bed and a blue-and-white rug from Portugal.*

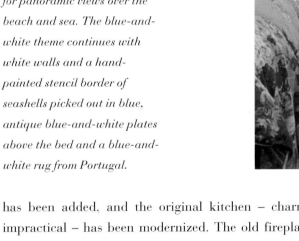

has been added, and the original kitchen – charming but impractical – has been modernized. The old fireplace at the end of the sitting room, complete with the original bread oven, has, however, been retained.

Thick walls, and floors of quarry tiles dictate the simple decorative themes throughout: white walls, lime-washed beams, traditional panelling and handsome fabrics all create an attractive setting for a collection of nautical memorabilia.

One of the most outstanding features of this cottage are the extensive and striking views, and a stone seat built into the bay window of the sitting room provides a perfect point for observing the coastal wildlife.

Crown Cottage

CHELSEA • LONDON

Most of London's artisan cottages have been subjected to urban gentrification. This is one of the few to survive in something of its original form. Built in 1865 and still divided in two when the present owners acquired it several decades ago, only basic electricity and a single water pipe had been installed. The condition of the building was indisputably primitive.

Above: *The highly decorative Gothic folly-cum-summer house at the end of the garden, which is also a haven for salvaged gravestones and autumn spiders.*

Right: *A corner of the garden room with a Gothic "Cabinet of Curiosities". The contents of this treasure trove have been assembled by the owner from every corner of Britain over decades of knowledgeable collecting – with an especially keen eye for Gothic treasures.*

It is evident that when the cottage was built – perhaps by a thrifty local craftsman – second-hand salvage materials were used, which explains why the cottage seems even older than it is. Floorboards and roof timbers are notched, and odd bricks and whitewash were exposed when the old plaster was hacked off the walls. Stripping the staircase revealed that it was probably part of a second-hand structure. Even the doors and the windows had come from an earlier building. Beneath the old wallpaper there was

evidence of serious fire damage to the building in the past.

The cottage was replumbed and rewired, and a central heating system was installed before restoration work began. Many of the materials – especially authentic mid-Victorian doors and ironwork – were found in skips, salvage yards and junk shops, and great efforts were made to match period and scale to the original building. Cupboards, made from old doors, were built to fit, and the dining room fireplace was constructed from a variety of materials, including slate from a demolished site in the City, stone from a skip in South Kensington, pilasters made from scraps of timber, and a white marbled shelf rescued from a nearby house.

The low ceilings, basic proportions and original character of the cottage have been treated with respect, hence the exposed floorboards, soft blue-grey woodwork and whitewashed walls. Only the dining room, painted in bright 18th-century green, is an inoffensive deviation from the period.

In the sitting room the fireplace has been centred against the wall and the alcoves on either side fitted with shelves: the differing dimensions of the alcoves were successfully disguised by careful adjustments to the architraves of the shelves.

In order to preserve the dining room, an existing ground-floor bathroom was converted into a minimal galley kitchen, and the bathroom was relocated upstairs.

At the far end of the long, narrow garden is a folly-cum-summerhouse topped with a weather vane made from an old aluminium saucepan. Plants with their own indigenous backgrounds – bay trees from Florence, rosemary from Tuscany and rose bushes from Ireland – create a lush and pleasant "Garden of Memorabilia".

Left: *The sitting room of the cottage is based on a restful yet colourful unity of whitewash and unbleached calico curtains, which provides an ideal background for the chimneypiece, always the heart of a room.*

Above: *A veritable "treasure cupboard" is to be found in one corner of the sitting-room, attractively filled with decorative mementoes collected during holidays over the last 50 years, including Goldfinch and Donegal pieces plus a latter-day 1995 Peahen.*

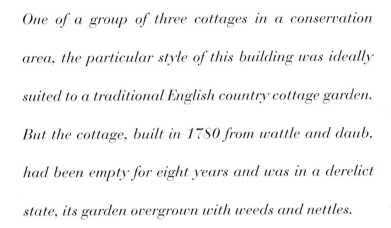

Church Cottage

STEEPLE BUMPSTEAD • SUFFOLK

One of a group of three cottages in a conservation area, the particular style of this building was ideally suited to a traditional English country cottage garden. But the cottage, built in 1780 from wattle and daub, had been empty for eight years and was in a derelict state, its garden overgrown with weeds and nettles.

The present owners had no plans to buy a cottage until, during a visit to friends nearby, they were told about this property. Despite its dilapidated condition they were charmed by the place, which they perceived as having a great deal of potential as a comfortable weekend home.

These keen and knowledgeable garden enthusiasts chose, unusually, to make the garden the starting point of the renovation. Weeds and rubble were cleared away, fresh topsoil was laid and planted with lupins, delphiniums, hollyhocks, alliums, roses, and other plants native to the traditional cottage garden. The perimeter of the property was bordered with a white picket fence, and a mellow brick path edged with lavender and roses leads to the wooden porch with its stable door entrance – one of the many visual links between the house and the garden.

The interior of the cottage had been altered over the years

Left and above: *The densely planted flowerbed facing the cottage includes achillea, Delphinium "Sir Galahad", Papaver orientale, Paeonia Duchesse de Nemours and Rosa Ferdinand Pichard. Perched on a bamboo stake is a folk art windchime from Gordon Bennet, a craft and garden store in San Francisco. On a rustic perch is a New England Dutch Barn bird house.*

and included extensions to the rear and side, which provided a kitchen and bathroom to the property.

The latest alterations involved repositioning the small staircase leading to the upper floor, moving it to the back of the cottage in order to create more space downstairs, and an open-plan reception area. The cottage was also rewired, replumbed, and a central heating system was installed.

Additional space was gained by converting the barn – the only survivor of the original garden – into a study. The barn was dismantled piece by piece and carefully reconstructed. But as the cottage is in a conservation area, and alterations are therefore subject to planning consent, the authorities insisted on a large and unnecessary window to be installed in the barn, which has been cleverly disguised by shutters and, appropriately, climbing plants.

Left: *The dining-table, chairs and dresser were commissioned locally: the oak used was reclaimed from the hurricane of 1987, which devastated the nearby forest. The spoon rack shows a collection of English, French and German spoons, dating from the mid-18th century. The 90-piece ironstone dinner service and the pair of lustreware biscuit barrels date from the 1950s. One barrel was found in a junk shop, the other in an antique shop in Galway, Ireland.*

Right: *The restored barn with the exposed timbers exactly as the originals were located. The shelving of reclaimed oak houses various collections, from gardening reference books and* Country Life *magazines, to local hand-crafted ducks, papier-mâché cows and French confit jars. Sofas are covered in horse blankets, paisley shawls and chenille rugs from London, Suffolk and even Madison Avenue. Lighting is provided by a hand-painted watering can, converted and complemented by a generous vellum shade.*

Left: One of a pair of handsome verdigris benches basks in sunshine flanked by Victorian chimney stacks, now planted with scented geranium. Trailing fuschia and begonia grow in densely planted terracotta pots. The herringbone path was laid using reclaimed bricks and has mellowed quickly to enhance the brickwork of the cottage.

Right: View through to the restored barn. Glazed awning pots of cosmos and chrysanthemum, underplanted with scented verbena, line up with well-used watering cans and gardening tools acquired from local antiques fairs. The timber-clad barn provides a strong background for an attractive display of Hosta sieboldiana elegans *and althea.*

Mustard Pot Hall

This unusual cottage, with its eccentric chimney stack, is set on top of a hill on the East Anglian coast. The original provenance of the building remains a mystery. Was it built as a folly, a dower house, or simply as a prospect cottage? The present owner – a designer and mural painter – believes that it was built by a local nobleman who inherited the estate in 1634, and probably built the cottage a year or so later as a retreat from the formalities of life in the Hall.

Above: *The brick cottage with its commanding chimney tower was originally built as an "eye-catcher". The original owner's initials "T.R." appear in wrought iron over the upper window.*

Right: *The red walls of the first-floor drawing-room are embellished with trompe-l'œil panelling painted by the owner. The original plaster ceiling coving has also been restored by the owner.*

The two storey cottage has a high attic, used as a spare bedroom, with magnificent views of the coast. There was already an extension to the rear, providing a large kitchen and entrance lobby, before the latest renovations began twenty years ago.

The ground floor ceilings which had been extensively damaged by fire were restored to their original state – a massive undertaking given that the ceilings are one of the

Left: *In the dining-room the walls are painted pale duck-egg blue with simple panelling. The design is taken from a 17th-century memorial tablet in the local church. In the centre of the room is a Charles II gate-leg table with a set of late 18th-century balloon-back chairs. Lighting is mainly by candlelight: hence elaborate metal wall-sconces and an 18th-century glass chandelier.*

Below: *The walls of the main bedroom, which overlooks the garden, are covered with a yellow-on-yellow striped wallpaper. The bed is mid-19th century and painted Prussian blue. Wall-sconces are of Regency origin. The bedside cabinet is from the Hepplewhite period and belonged to the owner's grandmother.*

Above: *The neo-classical bathroom has the exotic addition of Chinese Chippendale-style windows, designed by a cabinet-maker. The mildly domed ceiling was made by local craftsmen from curved plywood, and the decorative cornice of spheres by Romany Gypsies. The rose over the window comes from the owner's collection of classical plaster casts. The Victorian cast-iron bath is commodious and substantial while the toilet seat is an 18th-century carved Mendlesson chair. The wallpaper is a neutral colour; the curtains are made from an elegant* toile de jouy *fabric.*

distinctive features of this cottage. The hall, a long narrow corridor, sets the scene with its oak-grained Jacobean style mouldings and exotically patterned wallpaper. The dining room on the ground floor and the sitting room above are both embellished with period mouldings and friezes. The bathroom has a coved ceiling with a cornice of white balls, a notion prompted by a commission carried out at the Soane Museum in London's Lincoln's Inn. To reproduce the effect here, itinerant Romany gypsies were retained to hand-turn the hundreds of small spheres of curved plywood.

Fireplaces were unblocked and revived, and each room was painted and decorated in authentic 17th-century style. The owner's scholarly pleasure in period decoration is evident throughout, with results that a visitor to an English country cottage might not expect – for this is no conventional country retreat in which to relax and curl up in front of the fire. Where one might expect comfortable sofas and restful armchairs there are, instead, high-backed chairs around a gate-leg table, establishing a grander and more formal decorative manner. The only concessions in this very atypical country cottage are the modern plumbing, electricity and heating.

Left: *The spacious kitchen
faces south, overlooking the
garden, and was converted
from what were originally two
small rooms. After the partition
wall had been removed the
owner installed a set of estate
windows handsomely set
within the deep walls – deep
even for a traditional cottage.
The late 19th-century hand-
painted chairs, acquired from
a local antiques dealer, come
from Friesland, a village in
Holland specializing in
painted furniture. Twelve
guests can now be
accommodated. At one end of
the room French windows lead
into the garden. The 1920s
Lutyens-style table is graced
by a pretty blue-and-white
checked cloth. The floor is
covered with modern French
Provençal tiles. On the walls,
framed and mounted stuffed
birds are part of an ever-
growing collection.*

Paradise Cottage

YARCOMBE • SOMERSET

This 17th-century two-up two-down archetypal stone cottage, with roses around the porch and a large garden with old fruit trees, was virtually derelict and about to be demolished when it was bought by a member of an established local farming family thirty years ago.

Above: *The early 17th-century cottage was constructed of local stone in Bread Street – once famous for breadmaking. Grain was stored in an old barn at the adjacent cross-roads. The informal garden has roses and honeysuckle plus terracotta pots filled with colourful geraniums.*

Right: *A view of one corner of the sitting room with a comfortable sofa and old books piled high on an adjacent shelf. The window looks directly on to the garden. Jugs filled with flowers and china are displayed on the window sill. The simple green cotton curtains were made by the owner.*

The tiny cottage had just one room on either side of a steep staircase leading to three small bedrooms. On one side of the cottage, in a small lean-to with a large old-fashioned water heater, was an ancient wash house.

Sympathetic renovation was needed to accommodate a family of four without compromising the rural character of the property. A new staircase was built at the back of the house, and a wall on the ground floor was taken down in order to create a larger sitting room. At one end of the house a spacious family kitchen, which also serves as the main entrance, was added to replace the existing lean-to.

Left: *The sitting room exemplifies the owner's keen eye for colour and objets de charme. Furniture, pictures and china have been picked up at jumble sales and second-hand shops – chips or cracks did not really matter, as long as the object appealed. The sofas and chairs, covered in a variety of old chintzy linens with lace back panels and arm covers, are a mish-mash of styles and shapes.*

In addition to the structural renovations, all of the basic services required updating. Walls were replastered and painted in beige tones to give the interior plenty of light.

The spirit of cottage life has been captured in the furnishings and decorations: old pine settles and dressers, well-worn sofas and armchairs with remnants of old lace spread over the backs and arms, old quilts, paintings of country scenes, embroidery, religious texts, inexpensive ornaments and bric-a-brac, all found locally at jumble sales, charity shops and antiques fairs around the West Country, reinforce the impression of an English country cottage at its traditional best.

Comfort is the key. Walls are lined with pretty pictures and old china while shelves hold old books and memorabilia. Touches of bright pink on the floor and in the upholstery ensure warmth at all times. The piano at the far end of the sitting room is frequently played by the owner and is used for carol and hymn singing. Here, nothing is calculated. The unplanned decoration is simply the result of forty years of avid collecting. Outside, the old fruit trees flourish and the garden is filled with geraniums, sweet-smelling honeysuckle and roses – the perfect place to sip tea on an English summer afternoon.

Right: The kitchen was built on to the original cottage in 1974 when an old lean-to wash-house was pulled down. The walls were painted white and simple hand-made units were made using old pine. Panels of old lace are used to conceal pots and pans hidden beneath the sink. A tongue-and-groove stable door leads into the garden. The wooden floor is strewn with old rag rugs. To the right is a comfortable armchair upholstered in faded linen and covered with oddments of lace and embroidery. Every surface and wallspace is covered with china and objects, almost all of them relating to chickens or flowers.

Hilltop Mount

Perched on a Sussex hilltop in a large rural estate, this mid-19th-century farm-worker's cottage was only one room wide, very cramped and rather dark. But in generally good condition, and a reasonable distance from London, it made an ideal weekend retreat.

Basic amenities needed to be updated, and the modest period features reinstated. Replicas of early traditional cottage windows were installed, and new wooden doors were hung throughout. The original architectural features have been mostly retained, for example, fireplaces, the recesses to the sides of which are used for storage. The aim was to create comfortable interiors, simply furnished against a background of pale restful colours.

The small ground-floor sitting room led to an equally small dining room and kitchen. The narrowness of these spaces were addressed in a simple and imaginative way: a narrow clapboard extension – painted black to imitate a Sussex barn – running the full length of the cottage. This solution has led to the creation of a long airy walkway, with a new front door at one end and doors leading into the reception rooms along the inner side. Large windows built into the outer walls overlook an enchanting courtyard garden.

Above: *On the painted cream wall above the Aga cooker, between the hardwood worksurface and the wall unit, is a shelf especially designed to house olive oil bottles. Directly behind the bottles is a painting of a trio of Scottie dogs.*

Right: *The kitchen is the heart of the house with its lavish farmhouse appeal and cream-coloured walls. The Aga cooker and handsome hand-made tongue-and-groove cupboards were introduced into the new extension after the kitchen was enlarged. In the centre of the room is a pine refectory table surrounded by assorted pine chairs.*

Left: *The sitting room is small and very cozy. The walls are painted crushed raspberry red. On the walls are paintings – including many Victorian canine subjects – from the owner's growing collection. The floor is covered with sisal matting with a colourful rug on top.*

Right: *View from the kitchen through the lobby and into the sitting room. Throughout the house new tongue-and-groove doors were specially designed to fit the new openings. On the left is an old pine dresser, its shelves crammed with cookery books, antique and modern china, glass and a variety of memorabilia from far and wide.*

Left: *The ground-floor cloakroom is situated at the far end of the new walkway. Here the walls are lined with slatted Canadian pine painted white. The "thunderbox" is made from old cedar and the handsome washbasin, together with the chrome taps, came from the Ritz Hotel in London when it was undergoing refurbishment. Pictures – mostly from junk shops – are casually grouped together for effect.*

Right: *Upstairs, the main guest bedroom has plain white-painted walls and simple fine cotton voile curtains. The brass and iron bed is Victorian with its original frame to which fine muslin curtains have been fixed. The red-and-white checked quilt is 19th-century American. Among the wall paintings there is one of Queen Victoria aloft in a balloon.*

The wall between the dining room and kitchen was knocked down to make room for a spacious farmhouse-style kitchen. A conservatory, running almost the full length of the opposite side of the house, was added, with two sets of double doors linking it to both the kitchen and the sitting room. Two derelict sheds and an old barn at one end of the cottage were also linked to the main building and converted into two guest bedrooms and a studio. These extensions, too, were given clapboard exteriors to create a sense of unity and continuity.

These rearrangements and revisions resulted in a virtual doubling of the reception area, and neatly incorporated the conservatory, with its aromatic potted and climbing plants, which makes a seamless connection to the garden. Comfortable seating in this area overlooks the garden, while at the far end of the room, next to the kitchen, is the dining area.

The southern outlook of the cottage, leading into the fields, is a wild side to the garden with expanses of long grass. Elsewhere, climbing roses, honeysuckle and clematis form a colourful background for herbaceous borders filled with traditional cottage-garden perennials.

Flint Cottage

MIDDLETON • NORFOLK

The flint façades of these mid-18th-century two-up, two-down cottages were constructed with stones gathered from fields by local mothers and children who were paid "a halfpenny a bushel". Originally a terrace of four dwellings, the structures were subsequently arranged into a pair of Victorian cottages. The present owners – both artists – bought half the property, with an option on the other half when it became vacant.

Above: *The exterior of the flint and brick cottage, showing the doorway that leads into the dining room.*

Left: *The sitting room, frequently referred to as the "book room", is also used for musical entertainment, since the owner and his daughter are both talented musicians.*

Within days of the purchase, the local council issued a closing order deeming the cottages unfit for human habitation (the previous owner was an eccentric lady with 90 cats). Permission to live there would be dependent on the results of a long list of grant-assisted repairs.

Instead of spending the grant on installing a modern electricity and water supply, as suggested by the council, the owners chose to put in a powerful generator and spent their funds on a new roof and a bathroom.

Right: *A view through the arched double doors of the sitting room towards the hall and the new staircase. Here the decorative theme is based on a riot of jewel-like colours beginning in the sitting room, where bold turquoise walls and yellow ochre doors lead on to crushed strawberry walls in the hall. The staircase was painted by a local artist who embellished the sides of the treads with antique plaster roses painted a subtle shade of blue. On the far side of the staircase the recessed window is a glazed backdrop for a glorious display of coloured glass objects, casting colourful rays whenever daylight or moonlight shines through. To the right of the sitting room doors is the owners' splendid display of shell objects. The collection, initiated on a trip to Venice in the 1960s, is displayed on a painted side-table. Above the table is a display of tissue-paper flowers.*

Walls, woodwork and windows were repaired or replaced. A cramped stairway was removed in favour of a larger version which allowed more light and was therefore considered to be worth the modest loss of space. Two of the rooms on the ground floor were knocked into one to create a long narrow sitting room – known as the "book room". Upstairs, a spacious studio, a guest house and a bathroom were added.

Throughout the cottage, the walls are painted in bold colours and lined with dozens of paintings – mostly by the owners themselves and their friends. Old Persian rugs piled one on top of another set off the painted furniture and the collections of pottery, glass and shells.

Unusually for a cottage, the designs for the gardens verge on the grandiose, modelled on those of the Sissinghurst Estate in Kent. Within a magnificent pair of large iron gates, rescued from a demolition site in London, and bordered by a substantial stone wall (replacing a corrugated iron fence), are hundreds of rare plants, and one of the finest collections of snowdrops in the country.

Left: *In the breakfast room the one-time stable door, now glazed, leads directly into the garden. The circular 18th-century Dutch painted table in the centre of the room was found in a local antiques shop. The 19th-century glass chandelier is Venetian.*

Below: *The enchanting cottage garden glimpsed through the iron gates.*

Rose Cottage

PIDDLETRENTHIDE • DORSET

The owners of this delightful property in Dorset had been seeking a traditional unmodernized cottage, and this mellow brick cottage in a tranquil setting suited their requirements completely. The cottage, part of a pair built around 1840, was one of a quartet situated at the four extremities of a large estate.

O ver the years, the new owners spent weekends and holidays in the cottage despite the lack of electricity and central heating. Gas lamps provided light, the large inglenook fireplace heat, and the refrigerator and stove were powered by a gas cylinder outside the back door.

Twenty two years later, the second cottage, with which theirs was paired, became vacant. The delighted owners bought the neighbouring cottage and converted the pair into a single dwelling.

Apart from the addition of Gothic windows and a new door, the exteriors remained as they were. The interiors, however, were gutted and refurbished throughout. A new roof, central heating, two new bathrooms and a modern kitchen were

Left: *The size of the lobby was dictated by the size of the adjacent chimney stack. Despite its spatial limitations, however, it sets the decorative theme for the rest of the cottage. Here colour, flair and a basic disdain for conventional rules are manifest: a crowded home for walking-sticks and umbrellas, an oversized but perfectly poised cache pot and even a mirror.*

Above: *The old pine dresser in the kitchen (left) is loaded with a colourful assortment of china and family memorabilia. The walls of the hall (right) are papered with a modern version of an 18th-century design, which acts as a decorative backdrop for a favourite painting flanked by a pair of oval brass frames. The chest of drawers is partnered by a pair of Bentwood chairs.*

installed, but neither the modernization, nor the growing collection of furniture and *objets d'art*, have diminished the character or the rural ambience of the cottage.

Today, the spacious hall, once part of the second cottage, has a galleried stairwell. The sitting room has been greatly enlarged by incorporating the space previously occupied by the old kitchen and bathroom. On the opposite side of the hall, the kitchen and adjoining dining areas have direct access to the garden. A small rear extension provides a rather more formal dining room, and a cozy study.

On the upper floor, two of the original bedrooms have been

Right: Set against a background of pale green and soft pink, a wide variety of patterns and colours have been used for the curtains, upholstery, cushions and trimmings. The initial impression gained by any visitor to this cottage is that the sitting room has that rarest of all decorative achievements: grandeur in a modest setting.

Left: Despite the cottage's humble origins, the owner clearly has an instinct for luxury. Nowhere is her collection of objets trouvés *and* achetés *more decoratively – even grandly – displayed than in the sitting room. Every tabletop and surface has its abundance of treasures collected over the years. Each wall is embellished with paintings and porcelain plates.*

Left: *The dining area has a long narrow table, which runs the full length of the room. Here shades of yellow establish an unusual but hugely successful colour scheme: the pretty print table cloth, for example, blends with the bold sill-length curtains.*

Right: *The L-shaped kitchen-dining area has panoramic views over the garden and distant hills. A cozy, warm quarry-tiled room with simple pine units hand-crafted by the local carpenter, plus a modern Aga cooker.*

retained, and the third has been converted into a small bathroom. An extra bedroom and bathroom have been built within the roof space above the new study.

The cottage is set within a classic English garden. In summer, the garden is ablaze with the colours of peonies, foxgloves, clematis, lavatera, saxifrage, and heavy with the scent of old-fashioned roses, lavender, catmint and herbs.

Cider-House Cottage

FOREST OF DEAN • GLOUCESTERSHIRE

This 19th-century cottage, one of a quartet built for workers in the stone quarries of the Forest of Dean, was the one-time cider house. The cottage is constructed of stone walls with a slate roof, and was at one end of a group of four.

The current owner – a potter – bought the cottage many years ago during a particularly harsh winter, undaunted by the snow-capped roof, freezing interior and dripping walls. The roof was reslated and, after the foundations were treated for dampness, the original stone floor was replaced with a combination of flagstones, red quarry tiles and reconstituted floorboards. Concealed roof beams were exposed, and the modern tiled fireplaces were ripped out to reveal the original inglenooks, complete with their stone lintels.

After the partition walls in the cottage had been knocked down, the generous space allowed for a large sitting room, a dining room and a kitchen. A short, steep flight of steps leads to three bedrooms and a bathroom.

Large expanses of sombre grey stone walls, even when contrasted with natural woods and pale colours, do nothing for cottages inclined to shadow. In order to lighten the space and bring out the quality and texture of the stone, the owner decided on a kaleidescope of colours, giving the interiors

Above: Colours – brilliant and bold – dominate the cottage interior. Here is the blue hallway, seen from the fancifully painted dining-room – all of which are the owner's own vivid creations. In the blue hallway can be seen an open fireplace and a metal steel chair. The floor is flagstone.

Right: The view from the dining-room looking into the kitchen. The antique pine dresser is hand-painted a bold shade of lilac and holds pieces of the owner's brightly coloured pottery. The kitchen units are painted bright blue with china rose-shaped handles.

bright, bold walls decorated with swirls, roses and sunflowers.

In the sitting room the walls were painted in alternating shades of blue, ranging from a yellow-based blue to a lavender blue, and the ceiling was painted in various shades of yellow. Along the floor, brightly painted red skirting boards were patterned with pink spots.

Cobalt-blue doors lead into the vibrantly decorated dining room, where yellow walls have been painted with gigantic pink, lavender and orange roses, and even the furniture has been painted – an elaborate gilded Georgian mirror is now vivid orange.

These interiors radiate a sense of warmth rather than the chilly atmosphere usually associated with stone. Outside the cottage are the kilns, to produce the pottery which further enhances the vibrant interior decor.

Left: *In the entrance hall walls have been hand-painted to look like Regency striped wallpaper. The chair was re-upholstered in a pale fabric. The 19th-century French writing-desk belonged to the owner's grandmother.*

Right: *The blue sitting room with painted orange fireplace. The small blue chair with rush seat set in the empty fireplace was a gift from an Irish friend. The white wall cupboard, also painted by the owner, contains a collection of brightly coloured pottery. The green chair was reupholstered and also painted by the owner.*

Folly Cottage

HALFORD • WARWICKSHIRE

Above: The mellow shades of the exterior of this enchanting 17th-century brick cottage are emphasized by the afternoon glow of a late autumn sunset.

Right: Sunlight streams through the sitting-room window, enhancing the shades of the faux marble fireplace and highlighting the rich burgundy silk of the 18th-century armchair.

Located in the grounds of an estate dominated by a magnificent early 18th-century Gothic mansion, this early 17th-century folly has been converted into a striking dwelling, and is a fine example of a bold approach to interior restoration. Comprehensively modernized and transformed as a home for the widowed estate owner, the ingenious structural innovations have resulted in a dramatically decorative interior.

Originally, the cottage was virtually one large room with the fireplace at one end and two tiny rooms off the other – in effect restricted spaces rather than functioning rooms. The cottage's electricity and water were updated, central heating was installed, and the original chimney stack was rebuilt. As the original brick floors were irreparably damaged and potentially hazardous, they were replaced with honey-toned Victorian floorbricks attractively laid in herringbone and linear patterns. Wooden beams were scrubbed, treated and sealed. New, but traditional, doors were introduced, and the existing windows were exchanged for a Gothic set from a local almshouse which was undergoing modernization at the same time.

Left: *The west end of the
sitting-room has exposed
beams and French windows,
which lead directly into the
garden. Here, bright red
painted walls and richly
coloured furnishing fabrics
accentuate the grandiose mood
and Gothic theme. The unusual
pelmet was inspired by the
shape of the windows and is the
handiwork of the owner. In the
centre of the room the large
Knoll sofa is upholstered in
burgundy velvet and strewn
with damask-covered cushions.
Seemingly overscaled furniture
such as the magnificent
Broadwood piano are
comfortably accommodated
within the limitations of the
cottage. On the floor, boldly
coloured rugs, laid one on top
of another, echo the strong
tones of the decoration. On
winter evenings the cottage is
cozy and warm with huge log
fires adding to the sense of
drama and grandeur.*

Below: *In the sitting-room is this Bishop of Lincoln's mid-Victorian throne, acquired by the owner's father. The piece is so vast that it reaches beyond the top of the pelmet board.*

The most spectacular decorative measure involved the accommodation of five thousand books from the owner's library. Floor-to-ceiling wooden bookshelves were built against the far end wall of the sitting room, and similar shelves were also built on either side of the fireplace at the opposite end of the room. Intended as an expedient solution to the storage of so many volumes, these book-lined walls are a dramatic feature of this imposing yet restful room.

Rich red walls and bright green paintwork suit both this unique library and the large pieces of furniture which include a grand piano, a huge Gothic chair and a handsome crystal chandelier.

In the summer months the interesting interior of this cottage is well matched by its exterior – a mass of climbing roses, various borders of colourful plants, and a large pond which is home to multitudes of wildlife.

Right: *One end of the kitchen as seen through a Norman arch. Here, a small pine dresser is crammed with antique blue-and-white china. The border of harebells was designed and painted by the owner.*

Waterside Cottage

BISHOPS CANNINGS • WILTSHIRE

Built in 1846 on the edge of a stream in a secret valley, this lichen-covered Gothic fantasy set in 100 acres was virtually derelict when it was acquired by the present owners who were searching for a remote property surrounded by water and wildlife.

The cottage had been clad with a porous stone called tufa. Tufa evolves from the process of natural spring water seeping through limestone and washing out a carbonate that hardens into the tufa, which remains light in weight and easy to saw. The Romans had used tufa extensively in the construction of their Roman villas and steam baths in this part of the country. The tufa used for building this *cottage orné* had given the exterior walls delightful warm biscuit tones. The interior, in contrast, was cold, dark and small.

But the listed estate cottage, once used as a lodge to accommodate a head-keeper and as a base for hunting and fishing expeditions, required the consent of Historic Buildings officials before any alterations could be made. After many months, it was agreed that the property could be extended at the rear to provide a new kitchen, cloakroom plus shower, and an entrance lobby. The addition of these elements gave the cottage more agreeable proportions as well as extra space.

Above: *The cottage, seen here from the far side of the pond, nestles in a hollow surrounded by woodland. The barge-boards, exterior doors and fenestration are painted blue to contrast with the tufa-clad exterior.*

Left: *The French windows of the small drawing-room open into the garden. Minimal curtains allow maximum light. The high wooden shelf around all four walls hold a variety of curiosities based on country pursuits.*

Below: A *Gothic-style*
bedhead and a patchwork
quilt made from offcuts of rare
fabric collected far and wide.
Pillows in subtle blue and
deep pink-patterned fabrics
establish a delightful contrast
with the cream-and-blue
painted furniture.

Right: *The main bathroom,*
which is located upstairs,
demonstrates the delightful
contrast gained by placing
sophisticated decoration in a
rural setting. Here, the chair
covering contrasts with the
simple tongue-and-groove
walls, enriched by the unusual
framed botanical prints.

Upstairs, the building remains exactly as it was: just enough space for a bedroom and bathroom.

A further official stipulation was that the new walls must be clad with tufa. Pieces of tufa were therefore gathered from the valley where generations of badgers had played with them and made them smooth, which provided the walls with stones of a smoother surface texture. The building was also given a new roof and an underfloor heating system.

Initially, the interior decorative themes were based on fishing and the river. But the owner's major business interests are concerned with fabric which he sources from all over the world, and his journeys to northern England and South Africa have provided appropriate furniture and modest *objets d'art* for the cottage. He credits these interesting finds to the poets and writers of the "Lakeland picturesque" movement, and to the affluent British ex-patriots who lived and died in South Africa, having furnished their homes with heirlooms from their mother country.

Classified as "A Site of Special Scientific Interest", the owner's land is a paradise of natural wildlife with acres of woodland and trout-filled streams. Badgers, deer, grey wagtails and green woodpeckers abound, and throughout the summer the fields around the cottage are full of wild flowers.

Sparrow's Cottage

CAVENDISH • SUFFOLK

Perhaps the most surprising fact about this cottage, first known in parish records as No 1, The Street, is that, despite its charms, the local villagers have long referred to it as "The Hovel".

Above: *From the window of the bathroom there is a delightful view of the garden. Pink walls, brown woodwork and antique natural linen curtains are the decorative theme. The Victorian doll's house is part of the owner's collection, assembled since childhood.*

Right: *In the dining-room, the owner's favourite room, the narrow table, originally belonging to a tavern, is partnered by a pine shelf, which displays a collection of decoy ducks, set against the cream wall.*

The cottage, in a small, sleepy Suffolk hamlet, was built in the early years of the 17th century. Throughout its history it has been home to a long list of local craftsmen most of whom have, in various ways, made their personal contributions to the structure and decoration of the building. These contributions were probably at their most positive in the early 19th century when the red-brick elevation and a lean-to at the rear of the cottage were added to give the building its present form.

One or two owners in the mid-20th century had also added some contemporary decorative touches. But the present owner – an American antiques dealer who spends several months of the year in rural England – removed the inappropriately tiled fireplaces, multiple layers of wallpaper and the unattractive linoleum floorcoverings.

Left: *The cozy seating area highlights the owner's zest for mixing textures and colours, ranging from the exposed floorbricks and simple country furniture to the upturned wicker laundry basket that doubles as a coffee table.*

Below: *In the kitchen, shelves and all available surfaces are covered with old storage jars and enamelled pots.*

Two-up and two-down is the domestic formula that has endured in Britain through the centuries, usually comprising two bedrooms upstairs and a small sitting room and adjacent dining room and kitchen downstairs. The original charms of the rooms have now been fully restored in this cottage and it is essentially as it was two centuries ago, except for the bathroom which has been incorporated into the ground floor lean-to.

The timber of the original doors and staircase has now been revealed, and the brick floor and immense inglenook fireplace renovated. Sunlight now filters down the chimney in the summer months, while in winter log fires keep the place warm and cozy. Even the plasterwork in the cottage is once again authentic, having been applied by local reeds rather than lath.

Using the modest proportions and shape of this cottage to its limits, the interiors are now uncluttered and simple. This style is well suited to the owner's collection of period

Left: *The simple iron bedstead in the single bedroom, dating from the turn of the century, was painted a soothing shade of green. The maplewood washstand acts as a side-table. The wickerwork child's chair, candleholder and green-and-white jug add their touches to a carefree miscellany.*

Right: *The main bedroom is located on one side of the upstairs hallway. Here, the floorboards are painted dark brown to link them with the rest of the woodwork. On the far wall a large armoire gives the room an unusual sense of scale and proportion.*

furniture, paintings, prints and pottery, as well as a highly personal collection of 19th-century wicker baskets and butter-moulds.

Outside, the front of the cottage has been painted pink while the brickwork at the back has been left bare. In the months of summer, the cottage walls are covered with climbing roses and clematis and bees buzz around groups of herb-filled terracotta pots arranged on the small terrace.

Downland View

FROXFIELD • WILTSHIRE

Originally built for the manager of a local chalk pit, this late Victorian cottage was virtually obliterated by a hideous lean-to tacked on to the front of the building. On first viewing the property, the new owner perceived it as a dreary little place with a dreary garden.

Above: *Two early Victorian tole student lamps, flank a much-loved but shattered Leeds ware teapot. French pots occupy the former fireplace in the kitchen.*

Right: *Behind the oak chair and circular table a Victorian oak cupboard, crossbanded in mahogany, is painted off-white inside and houses the owner's considerable collection of china.*

Beneath this offensive structure, however, was an enchanting two-up, two-down house. Late Victorian cottages tended to have larger rooms, higher ceilings and bigger windows than their earlier counterparts. In this particular cottage there was also a wide range of features – from fireplaces and door handles to curtain poles and cornicing – echoing a variety of architectural conventions. Although many of these were replaced by more authentic examples of the respective areas, the idea of being authentically "period" was considered unnecessary, and appropriate decorative themes were chosen to complement the present owner's personal collection of furniture, paintings and objects.

The particularly understanding transformation of this cottage involved replacing the make-do windows with those of a handsome Gothic design, and the ugly lean-to with an attractive porch. The old barn to one side of the cottage, which was once used as an artist's studio, was transformed into a spacious sitting room, its walls lined with wide tongue-and-groove panelling copied from a fragment found in a cupboard. A modest extension with a large Victorian fireplace was added to house the new kitchen, and the old cooking range was removed and a simpler version installed.

Upstairs, there is now an elegant bathroom, and the advantages of Victorian architecture are clearly apparent with the spacious bedrooms and high ceilings. *Trompe-l'oeil* panelling, waxed floorboards, painted furniture and colourful china accentuate the "country house" appeal, irrespective of purist doctrine. This is traditional English country house decoration at its most satisfying – both to eye and comfort. As the poet E. V. Lucas observed, the best of all domestic arrangements was "to live in a Victorian house opposite a Georgian house".

Outside, the garden has been modelled on a traditional 19th-century cottage garden with a topiary and a herb garden intermixed with colourful bedding plants, as well as bay trees to create a sense of scale and proportion. According to this owner, the secret of a successful cottage garden is to fill the beds with perennials and then, irrespective of colour or size, never dig them up.

Left: *A barn to one side of the cottage, which for decades had been used as an artist's studio, has been cleverly transformed into a sitting-room. The wide, beaded matchboarding of the walls has been retained, and the room enhanced by the installation of a handsome period fireplace. The rug in front of the hearth is a Kelim and the patchwork table cover is English Victorian. The lamp bases are converted spirit jars. The room holds a mix of English and Italian ceramics.*

The Gatehouse

SHELVE • SHROPSHIRE

Built around 1810, this three bedroom cottage was originally part of a large Hall belonging to the Church of England and used by missionaries as a rest home. The estate was sold in the mid-19th century, but the cottage was retained for the resident gardener and his wife, who later sold it to the present owner. For the new owner, this charming Regency property evoked memories of his parents' cottage in Northumberland, where he grew to know and cherish country life.

Above: *The garden of this long and narrow early 19th-century cottage combines the practicality of a well-stocked kitchen garden with a colourful abundance of pink, pale mauve and cream lupins with deep blue delphiniums. The trellis obelisks were made by the owner.*

Right: *Sunlight streams through the window on to the sleepy hound relaxing on his comfortable high-backed chair by the fire. The room's walls are a warming raspberry red colour and the floor is of local stone tiles, covered with colourful rugs. The corner cupboard houses lustre ware.*

From the lane, the building appears to be a conventionally attractive red-brick cottage. On the other side of the boundary wall, however, is the legacy left by generations of dedicated gardeners – large flowerbeds crammed with lupins, poppies, delphiniums, hollyhocks, Jacob's ladder, pink roses and campanula, standing out against the red bricks and white woodwork. Completing the rural scene, a resident assortment of chickens, lamb, cats, dogs and doves wander leisurely in these bucolic surroundings.

Left: *The cozy sitting-room has comfortable seating grouped around the fireplace. On the floor in front of the fire is a colourful Azabzzar rug bought in Istanbul. Most of the decorative accessories were found in local antique shops. An old-fashioned tongue-and-groove door leads to the stairs and the bedrooms above.*

Right: *The main guest bedroom, with a mahogany sleigh bed, has exposed wooden floorboards and bold yellow walls hung with botanical prints. Here, French and English furniture are combined with continental porcelain. Through the door, beyond a narrow lobby, is the owner's bedroom, which has been painted bright blue.*

The structural characteristics of a traditional country cottage were made an integral part of the present owner's overall decorative scheme. Newly plastered walls have been given a rough finish to make them appear older, while wooden doors have been painted in thick gloss. In the dining room the mellow brick floor was retained despite its uneven levels. In the kitchen new slate tiles were used, laid upside-down for a more rustic effect. The same was done in the sitting room and colourful rugs were added for warmth.

Throughout the cottage, bold colours such as deep terracotta, dark green and bright yellow have replaced the traditional magnolia. The one exception to this theme is the

kitchen, where cream walls offset the pine furniture. The sitting room, also on the ground floor, has darker, richer colours, providing a warm background.

Upstairs, the colours are equally bold but on a lighter scale to give brightness to the rooms. Here, yellow and blue walls complement rows of botanical prints, old lace, linen, continental porcelain and quilted eiderdowns.

Most of the furniture has been acquired through numerous visits to local junk shops and antique markets. Hence the abundant rugs, comfortable sofas and chairs, and the simple pine fireplace which embellishes the existing brick opening in the sitting room.

Left: *The traditional cottage kitchen has painted cream walls and a flagstone floor. An old pine table and a set of pine chairs add to the ideal country cottage kitchen ambience. An assortment of pots, pottery and china have been collected over the years by the owner on his travels around the countryside and abroad. The pastel portrait above the shelf on the left was found at a* Parisian marché aux puces. *The chicken, c. 1890, is one of a pair painted by a local artist.*

Right: *The original brick wall separating the Hall and cottage. In the distance is the* pigeonnier *made by a local craftsman. In the foreground is one of the owner's prized chickens with colourful fantails. The gravel path leads to a seating area for picnic meals. To the right, the path leads to a lavender walk where apple trees are being trained on to an espalier.*

The Ancient Cottage

NEAR BLUBBERHOUSES • NORTH YORKSHIRE

This 17th-century cottage was bought many years ago by the owners of the adjacent antique shop from the previous occupant – an old lady who was reputed to be a witch. The large hole piercing the peg-tiled roof was, according to the locals, used by the witch to fly in and out of her den.

Above: *A new Gothic-style window provides additional light for the stairwell.*

Right: *A view of the sitting-room, with its colourful textiles and rugs, looking through the kitchen into the garden. The collection of mocha ware is decoratively displayed in a 19th-century painted German cupboard. Favourites from the owner's collection of primitive pictures and pottery add their colourful touches to the walls of the room.*

The property had been neglected throughout, with old rags stuffed into every corner. Thick dark brown paint covered every surface and wall, and even the furniture. The condition of the cottage was, however, largely irrelevant to the new owners, who were using the space as a convenient storage unit for their business, until their daughter chose to convert it into a home for her own family.

The local clay, used extensively for building such dwellings at that time, had kept the cottage structurally sound over the centuries, and well insulated. The tall and narrow cottage, with one room on each of its three floors, was originally built around an enormous chimney stack. To one side of this, a simple wooden staircase winds upward to a large wooden board in the top floor, similar to a trap door, which can be lifted out when necessary to provide access for incoming furniture. On the other side of the chimney, on the ground floor, there was just enough space to install a tiny bathroom with loo, shower and basin.

Windows, doors, rotten floorboards – and the hole in the roof – were repaired or replaced. The ground floor was wholly renewed with old bricks laid square to the room rather than in the traditional herringbone pattern which would have made the space appear smaller. A small lean-to at the rear of the cottage was converted into a practical kitchen.

Unusual in an artisan's dwelling is the very fine quality of the beams, which pre-date the rest of the construction by two centuries. These came from Sir Robert Hitcham, a local nobleman and benefactor, who had already bequeathed money to a school and to almshouses and, before his death in 1634, authorized that unneeded sections of his 15th century castle should be used for renovating the homes of the poor.

In the bedrooms the strange geometric circles carved into the beams – like the thorns and shoes found in the chimney – were devices to ward off other witches and evil spirits.

Left: *In the tiny attic bedroom, a chest covered in French toile de jouy is flanked by a pair of Victorian iron bedsteads. Giant beams and elm floorboards add to this notable contrast of basic rusticity and sophisticated decoration. Perched on the pelmet board is a display of wooden decoys.*

Above: *The narrow stairwell winds around the great brick chimney stack. Natural materials such as old brickwork and different woods make for dramatic contrasts. Bookshelves have been built into a corner of the landing making use of every available inch of space.*

Evergreen Lodge

KEMBLE • GLOUCESTERSHIRE

Constructed from honey-coloured local stone this 17th-century cottage, set within a small dell overlooking a trout lake, is part of a sizeable estate in Gloucestershireshire.

Above: This pretty, 17th-century cottage built of local stone, is set by a lake on a large estate in Gloucestershire.

Right: Looking from the main sitting-dining room into the smaller room at the far end of the cottage. The refectory dining table with barley-sugar twist-turned legs was found locally.

Although the cottage has been restored and upgraded, the nearby poplar copse cast an almost permanent shadow over the property, rendering the rooms oppressively dark. Ultimately, the estate owner felled the trees, and also demolished an ugly breeze-block garage.

No structural alterations were needed to the cottage, but the new tenant – an interior designer – installed modern electricity, plumbing and heating. The wooden floorboards and low ceilings were retained and, indeed, emphasised rather than concealed.

A small utility room, housing the refrigerator and washing machine was grafted off, rather than on to, the entrance lobby, which remains essentially the entrance to "The Room" – the heart of this charming weekend home. "The Room" is quite large for a 17th-century cottage and provides relaxing seating arrangements as well as an adequate dining area which is conveniently adjacent to the small but functional modern kitchen. Another, smaller sitting room has also been skilfully incorporated into this scheme.

Left: *An unusual but practical adaptation of the "open plan" theme and undoubtedly the heart of the house, encompassing seating area, dining area and small kitchen. Shown here is a part of the sitting room, the far end of which is dedicated to the kitchen – the different functions denoted by floor tiles for one and exposed wooden boards for the other. This division is further accentuated by a painted cream-and-zinc workstation on the edge of the kitchen. Throughout the room the strong black-and-white theme predominates: plain white walls, black beams and black-and-white floor tiles. On one side of the room a painted cabinet houses the owner's collection of glass and china, while in the centre of the room comfortable armchairs are covered with pale calico. The window at the far end of the room overlooks the garden and fields beyond.*

Left: *In the guest bedroom is a profusion of white linen, white towelling and white cotton enlivened by subtle touches of blue and white such as the striped pillow cases and the checked bed valance. The walls are painted matt white and the tongue-and-groove doors are in white gloss.*

A dramatic matt black staircase leads upstairs, where everything is overwhelmingly white – white walls, glossy white woodwork and surrounds for the recessed windows, and an abundance of crisp, white linen.

Right: *The smaller sitting room, which is cozy and warm. In here a comfortable off-white sofa can be quickly transformed into a sofa-bed. For dinner parties, the table is moved into the centre of the room and folding chairs, hidden in a cupboard under the stairs, are brought out for the occasion.*

Monk's Retreat

*A group of six 16th-century whitewashed cottages –
originally rest houses for monks from a neighbouring
abbey – nestle virtually on the bank of a river in this
beautiful wooded valley in East Anglia. Devout
villagers were known to leave daily substance for the
monks outside their doors.*

When the abbey closed, a farmer bought the cottages
for his labourers, presumably at a favourable rate,
and the agricultural work-force moved in. Today,
after major renovations, the sextet of cottages is a trio of
cherished country homes for escapees from city life and work.

The largest cottage of the group, attractively rose-covered
and with its original doors, latches and handles still in
working order, certainly looked the part of the ideal country
retreat, but it was riddled with damp and lacked electricity
and heating.

Left: *The dining-room's pale
tones are emphasized by the
white mounts of the watercolours, which contrast with
practical country furniture:
early English elm chairs and a
French rural fruitwood table.
The domed Stilton cheese cover
is decorated with cows and
entwined mint leaves.*

Above: *Another view of the
room, here looking towards
the garden. The Regency pine
corner cupboard houses a
rare collection of lustre ware.
A collection of watercolours of
the Nile is partnered by a milk
maid's harness.*

Left: The entrance hall boldly upends quite a number of conventions by letting this invaluable space double-up as a second sitting-room. The day-bed is surrounded by a mixed collection of Victorian and contemporary cat pictures.

Right: The main bedroom is painted in Abbey white with an English toile de jouy, and decorated with a selection of samplers, an antique Durham quilt covers the antique brass bed.

The modern floor tiles were replaced by old flagstones, and the removal of two inappropriate fireplaces revealed a pair of charming inglenooks. Ceiling beams were sandblasted, and a small garden room was added on to the existing entrance hall. Light now floods the interior windows, which look out on views of the garden beyond.

An indoor, but well-glazed, open corridor now runs the length of the front of the house, while access to each of the three bedrooms is gained by three separate stairways. The low ceilings on this dark upper floor were beyond repair, and removed to expose the original beams which were in perfect condition. New dormer windows were installed in the bedrooms to provide more light.

The decorative treatment has been as comprehensive as the structural changes. Almost all the rooms in the cottage have been painted in soft shades of cream. Curtains are colourful chintzes and *toiles de jouy*. Walls are covered with samplers and watercolours. Pottery, china and other delightful objects decorate the dressers and shelves.

The country furniture, quilts, linens and lace, and collection of china and memorabilia, all contribute to the city-dweller's ideal of country cottage life.

Brickfields

COMPTON • SURREY

This spectacularly profiled cottage in Surrey was bought over 40 years ago by a noted potter and authority on 17th-century slipware. What had originally been a small one-and-a-half storey, thatched and timber-framed 16th-century hovel had been enlarged a century later. It subsequently became a brickyard and remained so until 1902 when it reverted to a private dwelling.

Today, as in the past, the kitchen is the heart of the house, and it still retains a rare timber-framed smoke chamber once used for smoking pork, concealed behind a ceiling hatch. A large window was installed in the kitchen to provide more light. This later gave the owner scope for decoration inspired by the strong greens, reds and blues of narrow boats and decorated with yellow ochre stencilling applied in the old-fashioned way, using waxed paper, yellow ochre pigment and distemper.

A range of kitchen utensils from bygone eras – knives, cleavers, cheese graters, apple peelers, cream makers, cucumber slicers, meat choppers and cherry stoners – are decorative as well as useful objects. The chandelier, made from

Above: *The inglenook fireplace dates from the 1660s.*

Left: *Collectors' corner within the cottage drawing-room, with an early 18th-century fiddlestick dresser, complete with a collection of European slipware.*

Right: *Here, giving a one-time mid-16th-century hovel a grandly flamboyant kitchen in the 20th century, is the table set for half a dozen guests. The sill of the window is decorated with a set of Brannam's milk pitchers from the turn of the century. To add to these decorative touches the kitchen is hung with chillies, garlic and herbs. The pots on both tables are the work of the owner. On the central table is a row of early kitchen slicers, the cream tones example is a rare apple slicer of the 1920s.*

Right: A blue-and-yellow cloakroom window opening on to the wild garden. The pelmet is a linen crochet c. 1900; the bobbly pots are Italian della Robbia *and the flower vase is modern Portuguese.*

an elaborately painted game larder decorated with dangling egg-whisks and strainers adds a whimsical touch to this room.

The sitting room has undergone a major transformation. At one stage in the cottage's history the sitting room and the kitchen were one, with a huge open fire built on to the back wall as this part of the house was too small to accommodate the conventional gable stack. Brick walls, constructed within the hearth, restrict its width and channel the smoke directly into the flue. The exposed joists of this colourful room are decorated with Swedish-inspired motifs, which match those stencilled on the walls.

At the rear of the cottage a small conservatory has been added. This makes a pleasant sitting area on summer evenings, as well as providing extra light in the hall.

This gabled cottage was built to withstand the weather, which explains the darkness of the interior. It seems strange now that little thought was given to the scenic views and wonderful sunsets.

Right: *In a bedroom, the blue ceiling and the colourful fire surround are decorated with hand-painted tassels. This feature was the work of the owner's son. A collection of Swiss ware on top of the surround add an additional unconventional touch. A French art deco fireside rug gives a cozy note to the scene and theme. White curtains at the window in this colourful room are hand-woven and delicately embroidered.*

In these remarkable surroundings Mary Wondrausch makes slipware pottery not only for the kitchen but also to commemorate family occasions. Her work can be seen in many museums, including the Victoria and Albert. Her shop is open Mondays to Fridays 9.00 to 1.00pm, 2.00 to 5.00pm. Saturday and Sunday 2.00 to 5.00pm.

Mary Wondrausch The Pottery, Brickfields, Compton, Nr. Guildford, Surrey GU3 1HZ 01483 414097

Spring Cottage

HIGH RODING • ESSEX

This century's shrinking of vast country estates has resulted in the release of many one-time estate cottages to the property market. Three hundred years ago this cottage was a one-room hovel. Today, it is the weekend home of an interior designer based in London.

Above: *A view of the dining-room. To mask irregularities the walls were covered with fabric and the woodwork was painted a pale greenish-blue. The fireplace is lined with 18th-century blue-and-white Delft tiles.*

Right: *The long and narrow hallway is painted in a light tone of green while the front door is a rich green colour. The floor has black-and-cream tiles and a Swedish side-table stands in the hall flanked by Gothic chairs.*

Many of the original features, such as the small cast-iron fireplaces in the bedrooms and the 19th-century cupboards, were still in good condition when the present owner bought the property. Other inherited features, however, were less appealing. The original stone floor in the hall had been taken up by a previous owner and replaced with linoleum. Each year during the summer, the hall becomes flooded with water – possibly from a spring. The water disappears as quickly as it appears, but no-one can explain why this happens.

Left: *The decorative theme of the study is exotically based on an old Turkish carpet, hence pinks and reds skilfully echoed in the curtains made from fabric with a design based on that of an old Paisley shawl. The handsome well-used and crowded 19th-century bureau is flanked on one side by a butler's tray-stand on which a collection of minerals from Morocco makes an unusual colourful display and, on the other side, an inviting armchair. An 18th-century side-chair provides eminently practical seating for coping with desk chores. On the walls, selected landscape paintings are part of a sizable on-going collection, including many "primitives" in which churches make a frequent appearance.*

Left: *A corner of the sitting-room. Inappropriate red bricks once lined the Edwardian fireplace but were removed and replaced by 18th-century manganese Delft tiles. The walls have been drag-painted pale orange. To the side of the fireplace is an 18th-century lacquered side-table with an Imari lamp. A collection of watercolours and a Regency mirror enliven the walls.*

Right: *The main bedroom is light and bright with two large windows overlooking the garden and countryside. The wallpaper has a nail-head border; the carpet is a blue-and-off-white patterned Brussels weave. A Victorian patchwork bedspread is partnered by an Edwardian chair.*

Apart from a new roof, little structural work was necessary. The brick fireplace in the sitting room was improved with a surround of English Delft tiles and a defunct Rayburn stove in the dining room was replaced with a cast-iron grate from a local school also surrounded by old blue-and-white tiles.

When the dining room ceiling was taken down for repairs all the beams, tie-bars and bolts relating to the original cottage were exposed. The walls were so irregular and in such bad condition that they were covered with fabric.

As a weekend home, the cottage has been furnished inexpensively with painted country furniture, Turkish kelims, patchwork quilts and a collection of china and *bric-à-brac*. The effect is simple and colourful, with pretty wallpapers and subtle tones throughout.

The bedrooms on the upper floor are small but charming. The largest, the master bedroom, is light and airy with two windows – an unusual feature in cottages of this size – which overlook the garden and surrounding countryside.

Outside, the garden – once dedicated to chickens and vegetables – is now a showpiece for roses and herbaceous borders with a large orchard and a huge raspberry cage, as well as neatly clipped topiary.

Penny's Cottage

NEAR NECTON • NORFOLK

Few medieval cottages have remained as entirely true to their past as the cottage pictured here, built around 1450 as a single-storey thatched dwelling with a dirt floor on the outskirts of a small village. This creeper-covered building was originally a timber-framed open hall house of the mid-15th century, before being altered in the mid-16th century.

Above: *At every point this once-medieval cottage has been modernized with skill, resulting in a building that hardly looks 20th century. This "modernization" entailed flooring over and transforming the structure into what might be termed a one-and-a-half storey cottage, which has proved ideal for contemporary escapees from the city.*

Right: *An ingenious and highly practical entrance to the kitchen via the leaf-covered porch. Here are folding oak shutters which can be used to cover the windows most efficiently. Every room, including the bedroom, is unusually snug, even on the most windswept of rainy nights.*

This mid-15th-century cottage consisted originally of just one floor 6 × 4 m (20 × 14 feet), and would have been heated by a wood fire, the smoke escaping through the rafters. It was built for, and probably by, a Mr Penny, the owner of 20 acres, and is still known as Penny's Cottage. A century later, another storey and a small parlour were added to the building, and a large inglenook fireplace and mullion windows were installed. Two centuries later, floorbricks were put down, later to be replaced by flagstones. None of these additions and changes have altered the cottage's medieval character.

Yet the cottage has had its historical ups and downs. The local population was virtually wiped out in the bubonic plague

Left: *This handsome time-piece is an authentic decorative touch for a practising horologist to add to any room. The dining area in the kitchen is cozy and inviting. The window to the right stands in the place of what was originally the entrance. Beyond, seen through the door, is a glimpse of the sitting room with its vast and comforting inglenook. The fireplace is well-provided with a collection of traditional long-handled cooking pots.*

of 1666 and the cottage was acquired by the Church, which still owns the land surrounding the property. The cottage, however, was returned by the Church to private ownership during this century.

When the present owner bought the cottage, it comprised of a large sitting room, a bedroom and a small parlour. The roof, windows and doors were all sound. Even the bedroom floor, mildly uneven, had been covered over with old oak boards. There was no evidence anywhere either of neglect or unacceptable "improvement".

The new owner added only a bathroom to make the cottage more habitable, and converted the parlour into a kitchen. The plaster wall between the old adjoining wood-shed and the sitting room was removed to make the wood-shed an integral part of the room.

The interior of the cottage is simple and historically correct: terracotta with dark brown ceilings and woodwork. The exterior has been rendered and painted dark brown, although cottages in this area were often decorated in strong shades of red or yellow ochre made from a traditional mixture of lime, milk and linseed oil.

The cottage is now almost completely hidden under a blanket of Virginia creeper, which covers the roof and most of the building. Unlike honeysuckle, which goes underneath the eaves and damages thatch, Virginia creeper has fine tendrils which attach themselves to the wire netting without disturbing the roof, effectively protecting it in summer when the straw becomes brittle and blows away.

Wealden Close

Above: This pretty 16th-century cottage has had its roof rethatched and the façade repainted yellow. Once a butcher's shop and a pub, the cottage is now a weekend and holiday retreat for a North London family.

Right: A view of the dining room – once the second parlour of the pub – where the present owners have installed their Rayburn stove. The principal parlour, which is now the sitting room is visible beyond. The floor tiles are original and the tapestry stool in the foreground was made by the owner's mother as a present to the house.

Before the present owner bought this late 16th-century Suffolk cottage some years ago, it had belonged to an antiques dealer who had, knowledgeably and sympathetically, restored and repaired the property.

Gothic windows were installed, salvaged from the village church in the 1970s, and a Gothic extension, still used as a conservatory, was also added. The tiled roof was replaced with thatch, and the damaged local pamment brick floor tiles were also replaced.

The new owner had little to do apart from inserting a few beams, and removing the bright red paint in the two upstairs bedrooms – the legacy of a former owner which had been retained for decorative effect. With her fine collection of furniture and paintings installed, this handsome cottage was immediately habitable.

The earlier history of the cottage is sketchy, although it seems to have been home to people of various occupations. It is believed that at one time it was a farm with a large orchard. Later the cottage was converted to a butcher's shop. In the 17th century a publican's licence was granted to the then-owner. The cottage-cum-inn had two parlours, one on either side of the front door, with thick walls and a huge brick chimney stack in between. Regulars were served from a small kitchen at the rear of the building where barrels of local ale were stored in a small cellar.

Right: *The bold red-striped bedcover in one of the bedrooms has been quite uninfluenced by the red paint that formerly decorated the first floor – thanks to the over-zealous publican.*

Left: *The house is now very much as it would have been in the 17th century when it was a pub, hence the somewhat primitive and informal kitchen.*

Years ago access to the first floor could be gained only by climbing a stepladder. Today, a handsome oak staircase winds around the chimney stack to the upstairs bedrooms. Part of one of the bedrooms has been appropriated to accommodate a bathroom and small landing.

Central heating had already been installed, fireplaces had been opened up, and a Rayburn stove put into the opening of the fireplace in the dining room. During the cold damp winter months, the vast chimney stack keeps the house comfortably dry and very warm.

Few ancient traditional cottages are so conveniently endowed for new owners, with all the modern amenities and devices in place.

Right: *The painted weather-boarded extension at the rear of the house was constructed by the previous owner in the 1960s. Hence the Gothic window frames, especially chosen for the kitchen, and rescued from the local village church. In the background the old barn is used for housing garden equipment and modern appliances, including a washing machine and tumble dryer. The brick and cobblestone path is constructed of local stone. The three-seater Edwardian garden bench is ideally situated for catching the early morning sun. Another option available during the summer months is the comfortable hammock strung between two old apple trees in the extension overlooking the garden, partly graced by a still-active orchard.*

Ivy Cottage

AMPTHILL • BEDFORDSHIRE

Until a couple of decades ago this 18th-century cottage was a derelict, tumble-down building set in a large unkempt garden. Empty for years, the bedroom ceilings had collapsed and the roof was propped up by posts.

Above: *The 18th-century dwelling has the appearance of a house rather than a cottage. The grand façade owes its origins to a mid-19th-century view that the front of the building should impress above all, while the rear was out of sight and therefore unimportant.*

Right: *View of the original fireplace as it was used for cooking and the long-established copper, which is still used today. The decorative tiles above the Rayburn stove, which supplanted an old bread oven, were bought from here and there by the owners.*

But the present owners wanted an unmodernized property set well back from the road with, above all, a large garden, so the neglected condition of the cottage was of minor importance.

The original structure had consisted of two cottages, built in 1790 from a hotchpotch of materials: wattle and daub, sticks, mud and clay. The property had been adapted to suit the needs of successive owners over the years and the end result was a building that was more house than cottage.

During the 1840s the cottage had been further upgraded, and given a brick fascia and two front doors – emphasizing its new status. At that time, it was considered important that the front of the house should look prosperous and the rear, since it was out of sight, did not really matter.

At the beginning of this century the cottage was named Ivy Cottage after Ivy Clarke, whose uncle was the local tailor. He had a small shop at one end of the cottage, while the schoolmaster rented a room at the other. The latter was a keen gardener and was even allotted a patch in the garden, which is still referred to as "Schoolmaster's Garden".

There was no bathroom, and heating and upstairs lighting were unavailable. Two power points had served the entire cottage. The new owners installed a bathroom within the space beneath the stairs, and the electricity was upgraded. Although many structures in the area suffer damage from dampness in the foundations, this cottage was absolutely dry even though the old floorbricks rested on a layer of sand and mud.

When the cottage subsequently became the owners' main residence, extra space was needed, and this was gained by incorporating the one-time tailor's shop and by adding an extension large enough for a kitchen and dining area.

The roof at the back of the house was raised in order to create extra headroom, and rotten beams were replaced. New windows, consistent with the somewhat grandiose cottage façade were made and installed by the 85-year-old local carpenter, who skilfully dealt with variants in the dimensions of the windows.

Outside, plans for the front garden were dictated by the existing box hedging. Common cottage flowers grow alongside rather grander and more unusual varieties, and the result is a well-ordered collection of colourful and aromatic plants.

Left: *The corner cupboard in the dining room was built when new chimney pieces were fitted for the house. The sturdy chairs are Victorian. The walls, in shades of ivory and pale yellow, are hung with prints ranging from railway posters to Victorian lithographs.*

Below: *A view of the cobblestone lean-to at the rear of the house, which is used for storing firewood, onions, shallots and other odds and ends.*

Captain's Ridge

WALMER • KENT

Above: *The white weatherboarded boatshed-workshop with adjoining upper-floor extension, the "boat balcony", which overlooks the garden.*

Right: *The old kitchen, now the new dining room, with the hanging model of a boat hull, plus bird models for table decor.*

This attractive Victorian cottage, situated on the outskirts of a small fishing village next to an estuary, which offers unusual fishing and sailing amenities, was built about a hundred years ago by a sea-captain who had decided to settle here.

Little had changed since the cottage was built in this small row, which offered magnificent views over the estuary to the sea beyond. Yet, as often happens in rural tradition, a second row of dwellings was built at a later date, completely blocking the view from the cottage. Thereafter decline set in.

The property had been empty for a decade when, eighteen years ago, it was bought by a sculptor of European birds, drawn to this part of the coast for the light and the extensive birdlife – the subject of his work.

The cottage had no bathroom and only an outside toilet. Despite this, and other flaws, the cottage had three potential bedrooms, a loft with an antique pulley for hoisting sails, and a spacious ground floor. Together with an understanding local builder, the sculptor repaired the cracked walls, and installed electricity, plumbing and central heating. An old washroom was converted into a dining area, and the three bedrooms were restored.

Right: *The owner's most
favoured room: workroom,
study, relaxation room. It is
also what is virtually a visitors'
exhibition room with ship
models and paintings galore,
from pier-head miniatures to
quite sizable models of a
variety of coastal and deep-
seagoing craft, taking over
almost every inch of wall space.
They represent a lifetime's
preoccupation with the "Age of
Sail". Most were acquired as
continuing extensions of a
passionately held youthful
hobby. Many are now museum
pieces, coveted by collectors
and curators alike. This room is
the perfect retreat, complete as
it is with the deepest armchair
in the cottage, television and
the daily papers, plus, of
course, work in progress.
Work here is mainly concerned
with rough sketches of bird
models which have aroused
the designer-modeller's
current interest.*

Left: *View of the highly individual bathroom – an extension which echoes the original tongue-and-groove walls in the rest of the original house. The most individual touch is the hand-painted seagoing sides of the bath, a creative spin-off from the owner's long-held maritime interest, which adds to the rare decorative touches throughout the rest of the house.*

Right: *Another addition to the original structure of the cottage, with more copy-cat tongue-and-groove authenticity and a perfect sky-blue finish. The proud ship's figure-head is a cherished household* objet d'art *and an unusual and decorative addition to any guest room. Again, there are more bird models – here on the side-table, to greet the dawn.*

Over the years, there have been further extensions and improvements to the property. A second sitting room has been intoduced, its shape inspired by a seagoing craft. A new and spacious bedroom and a second bathroom have also been added.

Many of the engaging original features have been retained, in particular the sitting room fireplace, and the pale blue walls in one of the bedrooms. The interior has been decorated with nautical memorabilia: antique sea-chests, two-dimensional ship models, naive pier-head paintings of seagoing craft, as well as both primitive and modern ornithological sculptures.

Inevitably, the exterior of the cottage has changed too. Above the boatshed and workshop, a loft extension housing the new bedroom has been added – referred to as the "boat balcony". It has been weatherboarded – in the manner of traditional coastal cladding – as have the other additions to this cottage.

Index

by location

First published in 1998 by
George Weidenfeld & Nicolson Limited

This paperback edition first published in 1999 by
Phoenix Illustrated
Orion Publishing Group, Orion House
5, Upper St. Martin's Lane
London WC2H 9EA

British Library Cataloguing-in-Publication Data
A catalogue record for this book is available from the British Library.

ISBN 0-75380-702-5

Edited by Jo Lethaby